The Golden Gate Bridge

Jeffrey Zuehlke

Lerner Publications Company
Minneapolis

For Gus,
spanner of
long distances

Lerner Publications Company
A division of Lerner Publishing Group, Inc.
241 First Avenue North
Minneapolis, MN 55401 U.S.A.

Website address: www.lernerbooks.com

Library of Congress Cataloging-in-Publication Data

Zuehlke, Jeffrey, 1968-
   The Golden Gate Bridge / by Jeffrey Zuehlke.
      p.   cm. — (Lightning bolt books™—famous places)
   Includes index.
   ISBN 978–0–8225–9407–9 (lib. bdg. : alk. paper)
   1. Golden Gate Bridge (San Francisco, Calif.)—Juvenile literature. I. Title.
   TG25.S225Z84 2010
   979.4'61—dc22   2008030641

Manufactured in the United States of America
1 2 3 4 5 6 — BP — 15 14 13 12 11 10

Contents

The Golden Gate Bridge

Have you ever seen
this famous bridge?

This is the Golden Gate Bridge.

It is one of the longest
bridges in the world.

The Golden
Gate Bridge

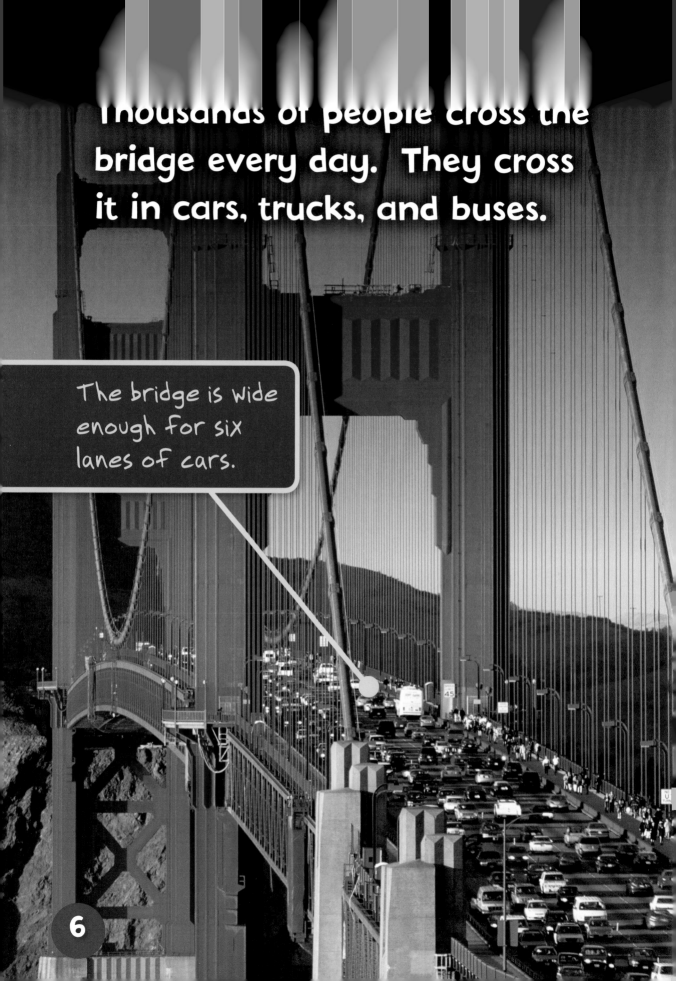

Thousands of people cross the bridge every day. They cross it in cars, trucks, and buses.

The bridge is wide enough for six lanes of cars.

Some people walk across the bridge. But it's a long walk!

The Golden Gate Bridge
is almost 2 miles
(3 kilometers) long.

Where is the Golden Gate Bridge?

The Golden Gate Bridge is in the state of California.

The bridge runs from the city of San Francisco to Marin County.

Marin County is on the left of the Golden Gate Bridge in this picture. San Francisco is on the other side of the bridge.

The bridge crosses a narrow strip of water called the Golden Gate. Can you guess where the bridge got its name?

The waters of the San Francisco Bay and the Pacific Ocean mix in the Golden Gate.

Can you see a
city in this picture?
This is San Francisco.

More than 775,000 people
live in this city. Many use the
Golden Gate Bridge every day.

These swooping cables hold up the bridge. The main cables are actually many cables wound together like rope.

How Does the Bridge Work?

The Golden Gate Bridge is a suspension bridge. That means cables hold it up. Two main cables run along the top. They swoop up and down from one end of the bridge to the other.

13

The main cables are connected to anchorages. An anchorage is a strong base that holds the cables in place. One anchorage sits at each end of the bridge.

This anchorage is on the San Francisco side of the bridge.

The bridge has two towers.
The main cables drape over
the tops of the towers.
The roadway runs
through the
towers.

The bridge's towers rise 746 feet (227 meters) above the water.

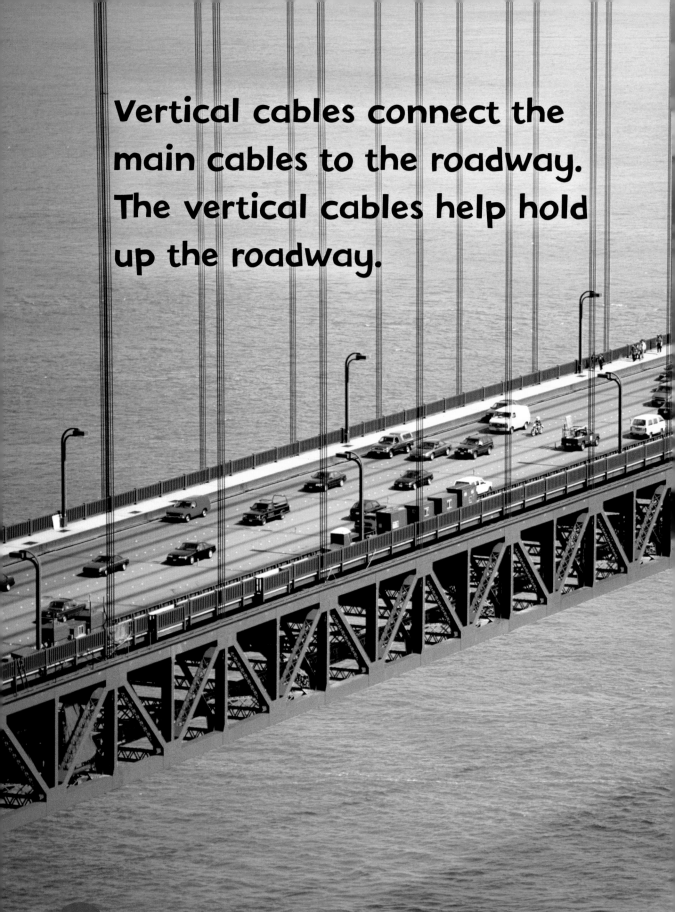

Vertical cables connect the main cables to the roadway. The vertical cables help hold up the roadway.

Vertical means "running up and down." The bridge has five hundred vertical cables.

18

Workers came from all over the United States to build the Golden Gate Bridge.

Building the Golden Gate Bridge

Workers built the Golden Gate Bridge in the 1930s. Thousands of them helped to do the job. They started work in 1933. They finished in 1937.

First, the workers used dynamite to blast holes in rock at the building site. Then they used cranes to dig out the loose rock.

A worker prepares to blast holes in rock. Rocky land lies at each end of the Golden Gate Bridge.

The workers filled the holes with concrete. Then they built the large, heavy anchorages. The main cables would be attached to the anchorages on each side of the bridge.

The anchorages are made of concrete. They hold the cables that hold up the bridge.

The towers were the next part of the job. Workers had to make holes in the rock under the water. Divers used bombs to blast holes in the rock.

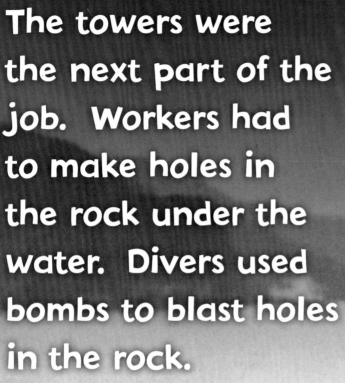

A diver prepares to enter the water.

Then workers built walls around the holes. They sucked out all the water. This gave them a dry place to work.

Workers built large concrete piers inside the dry area. Then they built the towers on top of the piers.

The towers are made of thousands of steel plates riveted, or bolted, together.

Each tower has about 600,000 rivets.

Workers built the roadway last. It is made of thousands of steel plates. The roadway is topped with concrete and asphalt.

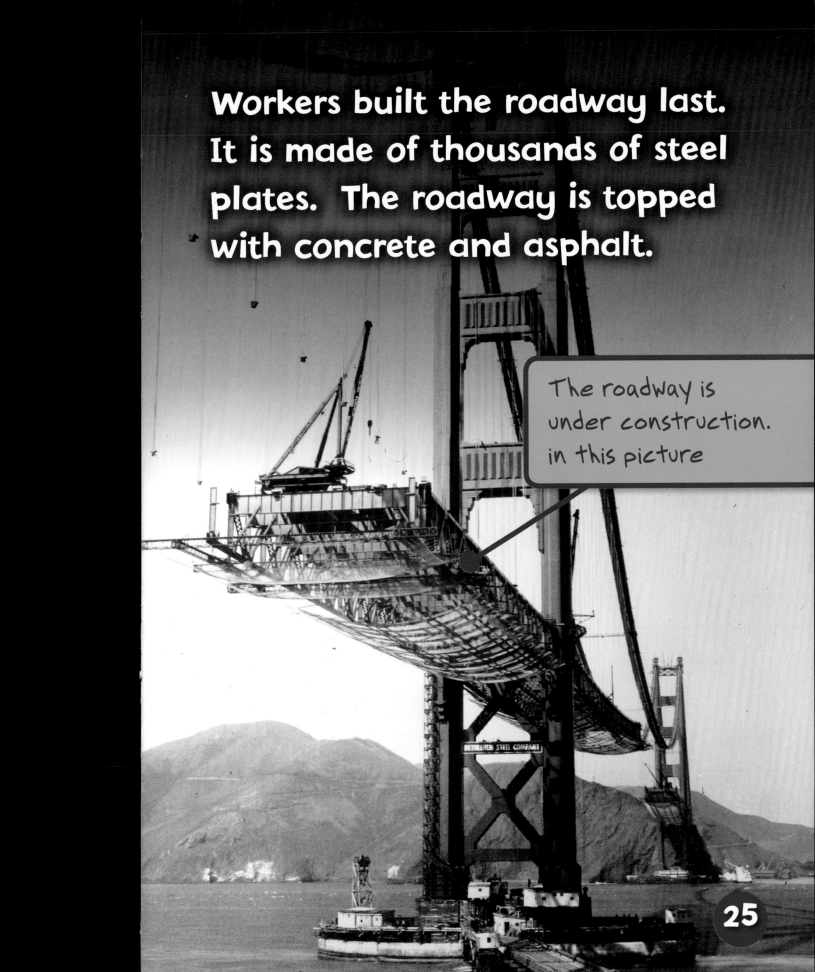

The roadway is under construction. in this picture

Workers finally finished the bridge in May 1937. It opened on May 27. More than 200,000 people came to celebrate!

Military planes flew overhead the day the bridge opened. Thousands of people walked across it.

More than seventy years later, people still celebrate this amazing bridge. It is one of the most beautiful bridges in the world.

The Golden Gate Bridge is painted orange. The exact name of the color is international orange.

San Francisco Bay Area

MARIN COUNTY

UNITED STATES

California

PACIFIC OCEAN

CALIFORNIA

San Francisco Bay

Golden Gate

Golden Gate Bridge

San Francisco

SAN FRANCISCO COUNTY

N

Inset Map

CALIFORNIA

San Francisco

PACIFIC OCEAN

0   1   2 Miles

0   1   2   3 Kilometers

Fun Facts

- About forty million vehicles cross the Golden Gate Bridge each year.

- Nearly two billion vehicles have crossed the bridge since it opened in 1937.

- When it opened, the Golden Gate Bridge was the longest suspension bridge in the world. Since then, people have built longer bridges. In the early 2000s, the Akashi-Kaikyo Bridge in Japan is the longest.

- A team of fifty-five workers keep the bridge safe and looking good. The team includes seventeen ironworkers. Their job is to replace old rivets and other metal parts. The thirty-eight painters keep the bridge looking like new.

- Southbound drivers pay a toll to cross the bridge. In 1937, the toll for one car was fifty cents. In 2008, the toll was six dollars.

- Between July 1, 2006, and June 30, 2007, the Golden Gate Bridge collected almost $85 million in tolls.

Glossary

anchorage: a strong base that holds cables for a suspension bridge

asphalt: a substance used to pave roads

cable: a strong wire that helps hold up a bridge

concrete: a hard substance made of sand, cement, gravel, and water

pier: a structure built to support a bridge

rivet: to bolt pieces of metal together. *Rivet* can also refer to the bolts used to hold metal objects together.

roadway: the part of a bridge that is used by traffic. This part of the bridge is also called the span.

suspension bridge: a bridge that is held up by cables

toll: a fee that people must pay to use some bridges, roads, and highways

vertical: running up and down

Further Reading

Britton, Tamara L. *The Golden Gate Bridge*. Edina, MN: Abdo, 2005.

Building Big: The Golden Gate Bridge
http://www.pbs.org/wgbh/buildingbig/wonder/structure/golden_gate.html

Fandel, Jennifer. *Golden Gate Bridge*. Mankato, MN: Creative Education, 2007.

Golden Gate Bridge
http://goldengatebridge.org

Zuehlke, Jeffrey. *The Hoover Dam*. Minneapolis: Lerner Publications Company, 2010.

Index

Photo Acknowledgments

The images in this book are used with the permission of: © David W. Hamilton/The Image Bank/Getty Images, pp. 4–5; © Livio Sinibaldi/Photodisc/Getty Images, p. 6; AP Photo/Paul Sakuma, 7; © age fotostock/SuperStock, pp. 8–9; © Andrea Pistolesi/The Image Bank/Getty Images, p. 10; © Jed Jacobsohn/Getty Images, p. 11; © Sam Clemens/Photographers Choice RF/Getty Images, p. 12; © Justin Sullivan/Getty Images, pp. 13, 31; © Joesph Sohm/The Image Works, p. 14; © Tom Paiva/Taxi/Getty Images, p. 15; © Harald Sund/Stone/Getty Images, pp. 16–17; The Redwood Empire Association, pp. 18, 19, 21, 24; © Moulin Studio Archives, p. 20; San Francisco History Center, San Francisco Public Library, pp. 22, 25; Courtesy of The Bancroft Library, University of California, Berkeley. Construction Photographs of the Golden Gate Bridge, #1905.14261 no. 1–114, p. 23; AP Photo, p. 26; © Michael Funk/Photographer's Choice/Getty Images, p. 27; © Laura Westlund/Independent Picture Service, p. 28.

Front cover: © Brian Lawrence/Photographer's Choice/Getty Images.